MW01036101

Better than Unconditional

Resources for Changing Lives

A Ministry of
THE CHRISTIAN COUNSELING AND
EDUCATIONAL FOUNDATION
Glenside, Pennsylvania

RCL Ministry Booklets
Susan Lutz, Series Editor

God's Love

Better than Unconditional

David Powlison

P&R PUBLISHING

P.O. BOX 817 • PHILLIPSBURG • NEW JERSEY 08865-0817

Scripture quotations are from the HOLY BIBLE, NEW
INTERNATIONAL VERSION®. NIV®. Copyright ©
1973, 1978, 1984 by International Bible Society. Used
by permission of Zondervan Publishing House. All
rights reserved.

Printed in the United States of America

ISBN 10: 0-87552-686-1
ISBN 13: 978-0-87552-686-7

Your love, O LORD, reaches to the
        heavens,
    your faithfulness to the skies.
Your righteousness is like the mighty
        mountains,
    your justice like the great deep.
O LORD, you preserve both man and
        beast.
    How priceless is your unfailing love!
Both high and low among men
    find refuge in the shadow of your
        wings.
They feast on the abundance of your
        house;
    you give them drink from your river
        of delights.
For with you is the fountain of life;
    in your light we see light.
Continue your love to those who
        know you,
    your righteousness to the upright in
        heart.

                    Psalm 36: 5–10

With these words, the psalmist David attempts to capture the wonder and power of God's love. It is something he wrote about frequently throughout his life. Yet, though he piles superlative upon superlative and pushes the limits of language, David seems to know that the love of God can never be adequately described in words. All he can do is invite others to come and taste for themselves.

Is it any different for us today? Is it any easier for us to talk about love—*any* kind of love— let alone the all-encompassing love of God? Certainly, God's love is something people are hungry to hear about. Yet in some ways, it's even harder for us to talk about it today, since most people now try to describe the most intimate, spiritual aspects of their lives in secular language. These words seem thin and pale and weak when they try to convey the richness and weight of a biblical truth. And nowhere is that more obvious than when it comes to God's love.

For example, have you ever had people tell you that God deals with his children with "unconditional love"? Most of the time, they are looking for a way to express how generous and complete his love is. But before we adopt this description we should remember David and ask: Is this explanation of divine love the best we can do?

I'd like to propose that God's love is much different and better than unconditional. Unconditional love, as most of us understand it, begins and ends with sympathy and empathy, with blanket acceptance. It accepts you as you are with no expectations. You in turn can take it or leave it.

But think about what God's love for you is like. God does not calmly gaze on you in benign affirmation. God cares too much to be unconditional in his love.

Watchful, Caring Love

Imagine yourself as a parent, watching your child playing in a group with other children. Perhaps you are observing your child in a nursery or a classroom, or on the playground, or in a soccer game. You might accurately say that you have unconditional love for all the children in the group. That is to say, you have no ill will towards any of them; you generally wish them well.

But when it comes to your own child, something more goes on. You take much more notice of your own child. Injury, danger, bullying or injustice arouses strong feelings of protection—because you love your child. If your child throws a tantrum or mistreats another child, you are again aroused to intervene—because you love. If your child thrives, you are filled with joy—again, because you love.

Of course, any of these reactions may be tainted by a parent's sin. Pride, fear of other's opinions, lust for success, superiority, ambition, or calloused self-absorption can warp parental love.

But imagine such reactions untainted by sin. Read Psalm 121, Hosea 11, Hosea 14, Isaiah 49, the life of Jesus. The Lord *watches* you. The Lord *cares*. What his children do and what happens to them *matter* to him. His watching, caring, and concern are intense. Complex. Specific. Personal. Unconditional love isn't nearly so good or compelling. In comparison it is detached, general, impersonal. God's love is much better than unconditional.

Active, Intrusive Love

God's love is active. He decided to love you when he could have justly condemned you. He's involved. He's merciful, not simply tolerant. He hates sin, yet pursues sinners by name. God is so committed to forgiving and changing you that he sent Jesus to die for you. He welcomes the poor in spirit with a shout and a feast. God is vastly patient and relentlessly persevering as he intrudes into your life.

God's love actively does you good. His love is full of blood, sweat, tears, and cries. He suffered for you. He fights for you, defending the afflicted. He fights *with* you, pursuing you in powerful tenderness so that he can change you. He's jealous, not detached. His sort of empathy and sympathy speaks out, with words of truth to set you free from sin and misery. He will discipline you as proof that he loves you. God himself comes to live in you, pouring out his Holy Spirit in your heart, so that you will know him. He puts out power and energy.

God's love has hate in it too: hatred for evil, whether done to you or by you. God's love demands that you respond to it: by believing, trusting, obeying, giving thanks with a joyful heart, working out your salvation with fear, delighting in the Lord.

In the C.S. Lewis's *The Chronicles of Narnia,* Lucy and her siblings were frightened at first to learn that Aslan, the Christ figure, was not a tame lion. But though he was not tame, they were reassured that he *was* good. In the same way, the Lord's love for his children is no tame love, no relational strategy. It's not characterized by calm detachment or a determination not to impose his values on you. His love is good in a way that's vigorous and complex.

That's the love that is poured out on you as his child, and you are meant—in some fashion—to have this same kind of love for one another: "Live a life of love, just as Christ loved us" (Eph. 5:2; cf. 4:32–5:2).

Such real love is hard to do. It is so different from "You're okay in my eyes. I accept you just because you're you, just as I accept everybody. I won't judge you or impose my values on you." Unconditional love feels safe, but the problem is that there is no power to it. When we ascribe unconditional love to God, we substitute a teddy bear for the king of the universe.

Love Has a Goal

What words will do to describe the love of God that is spectacularly accepting, yet opinionated, choosy, and intrusive?

> For Christ's love compels us, because we are convinced that one has died for all, and therefore all have died. And he died for all, that those who live should no longer live for themselves but for him who died for them and was raised again. (2 Cor. 5:14)

What words will do to describe the love of God that takes me just as I am but makes me over? That accepts people, yet has a lifelong agenda for change? Does it work to apply the label "unconditional love" to what God does—and to what godly parents and leaders are supposed to do, speak, and model?

The term seems flabby and weak in the face of God's powerful, purposeful love. However, many people do use the phrase "unconditional love" with good intentions, attempting to capture four significant and interrelated truths.

Four "Unconditional" Truths

First, it's certainly true that "conditional love" is a bad thing. It is not love at all, but an expression of the routine hatred and self-centeredness of the human heart. It's better to call it "conditional and manipulative approval." It plays capricious Lawgiver and Judge: "If you please me and jump through my hoops, I will smile favorably on you. If you displease me, I will either attack you or avoid you." People use the term "unconditional" as shorthand to contrast with manipulation, demand, or judgmentalism. They use it to shine the light on a sinful form of human relationship and to say, "Real love isn't like this."

Second, it's true that God's love is patient. He, and those who imitate him, forbear and endure with others in hope. God does not give up. Because God perseveres, his saints will persevere to the end and come through into glory. People use "unconditional" as shorthand for hanging in there through the process of change, rather than bailing out when the going gets rough. They use it to build hope over the long haul.

Third, it's true that true love is God's gift. It is at God's initiative and choice; it isn't given out on the basis of my performance. God's gospel love is not wages that I earn with a model life; it is a gift. It is a gift that I cannot earn; more than that, it is a gift that I do not even deserve. God loves weak, ungodly, sinful enemies. The gift is the *opposite* of what I deserve. God ought to kill me on the spot. Instead, he sent his Son to die in my place. People use "unconditional" as shorthand for such unearned blessing. They use it to overcome legalism.

Fourth, it's true that God receives you just as you are: sinful, suffering, confused. In street talk, he meets you where you are. You don't clean up your act and then come to God. You just come. People use "unconditional" as shorthand for God's invitation to dirty, broken people. They use it to overcome despair and fear that would shrink back from asking help from God and his people.

These are precious truths. They show that the adjective "unconditional" actually has a noble theological lineage in describing the grace of God. Unfortunately, the way people commonly use the term muddies the waters for four reasons.

Four Biblical Improvements

First, there are more biblical and vivid ways to capture each of the four truths just stated.

- The opposite of manipulation is not dispassionate complacency. Real love's kindness has zeal, self-sacrifice, and a call to change woven in (Isa. 49:15; 1 Thess. 2:7–12).
- The call for you to hang in there through the thick and thin of a person's struggles can be frankly stated: "Love is patient," "Be patient with them all" (1 Cor. 13:4; 1 Thess. 5:14).
- "Grace" and "gift" capture the free, unearned quality of God's love less ambiguously than "unconditional" (2 Cor. 9:15; Rom. 6:23; Eph. 2:4–10).
- God's welcome to the godless comes with a story attached: "Christ Jesus came into the world to save sinners" (1 Tim. 1:15). "Christ loved us and gave himself up for

us" (Eph. 5:2). The gospel is an action story, not simply an attitude of acceptance.

We do not need to use a vague, abstract word like unconditional when the Bible gives us more vivid and specific words, metaphors, and stories to describe what God's love is like.

Second, it is clear that unmerited grace is not strictly unconditional. While it's true that God's love does not depend upon what you do, it very much depends on what Jesus Christ did *for* you. In that sense, it is highly conditional. It cost Jesus his life.

In fact, the love of God described in the Bible requires the fulfillment of two conditions: perfect obedience and a sin-bearing substitute. Jesus, by his active obedience to the will of God, demonstrated and earned the verdict "righteous." His fulfillment of God's conditions is passed on to you when God justifies you.

And Jesus, in his passive obedience, suffered the penalty of death. The substitutionary Lamb took our death penalty to bring you freedom and life. So the love of God contains two "conditions fulfilled" as it is handed freely to you and to me. God's love contains both the life and death work of the One who was both God's servant and God's lamb. Unconditional love? No, something much better.

Third, God's grace is something more than unconditional in another way. It is intended to change the people who receive it. There *is* something wrong with you! From God's point of view, you not only need someone else to be killed in your place in order to be forgiven, you need to be transformed in order to be fit to live with. The word "unconditional" may be an acceptable way to express God's welcome, but it fails to communicate its purpose: a comprehensive and lifelong rehabilitation, learning "the holiness without which no one will see the Lord."

People often use the word "unconditional" to communicate an affirmation that "You're okay," robbing God's love (and a pastor's or parent's love) of its very purpose. You "turn" to receive God's love. You do nothing to receive blanket acceptance—and it doesn't take you anywhere.

Fourth, "unconditional love" carries a load of cultural baggage. As you've read the previous paragraphs, you've noticed how unconditional is wedded to words such as "tolerance, acceptance, affirmation, okay." It is wedded to a philosophy that says love should impose no values, expectations, or beliefs on another.

I could have used the technical phrase that arose within humanistic psychology: "unconditional positive regard." Most people think of this concept when they think of unconditional love: "Deep down you're okay; God accepts you just as you are. God smiles on you even if you don't jump through any hoops. You have intrinsic worth. God accepts you, warts and all. You can relax, bask in his smile, and let the basically good, real you emerge." This is a philosophy of life utterly at odds with God's real love.

Contraconditional Love

The opposite of conditional and judgmental might seem to be unconditional and affirming. The opposite of unreasonable expectations might seem to be no expectations at all. The opposite of being bossy might seem to be nondirective. Or so people wish.

Yes, conditional love is obviously hate, not

love. But unconditional love–used with the meaning the term now carries–is a more subtle deceit. It keeps company with teachings that say to people, "Peace, peace," when, from God's holy point of view, there is no peace (Jer. 23:14, 16).

If you receive blanket acceptance, you need no repentance. You just accept it. It fills you without humbling you. It relaxes you without upsetting you about yourself—or thrilling you about Christ. It lets you relax without reckoning with the anguish of Jesus on the cross. It is easy and undemanding. It does not insist on, or work at, changing you. It deceives you about both God and yourself.

We can do better. God does not accept me just as I am; he loves me *despite* how I am. He loves me just as *Jesus* is; he loves me enough to devote my life to renewing me in the image of Jesus.

This love is much, much, much better than unconditional! Perhaps we could call it *"contra*conditional" love. God has blessed me because his Son fulfilled the conditions I could never achieve. *Contrary* to what I deserve, he loves me. And now I can begin to change—

not because I can earn his love, but because I've already received it.

People who speak of unconditional love often mean well. A few use the words with the old theological meanings intact. Many just want people to care for each other. Many want to help those who view God as the Great Critic, whom they either serve grudgingly or flee because they can never please him. I have no doubt that the phrase has served some strugglers usefully, despite the riches it leaves out and the baggage it usually contains.

The Better Love of Jesus

But there is a good reason why the Bible tells us stories of amazing events, speaks in gripping metaphors, and unfolds detailed theology in order to inform us of God's love. It's because you need something better than unconditional love. You need the crown of thorns. You need the touch of life bestowed on the dead son of the widow of Nain. You need the promise to the repentant thief. You need to know, "I will never leave you nor forsake you." You need forgiveness. You need a Shepherd, a

Father, a Savior. You need to become like the One who loves you. You need the better love of Jesus. And by God's grace, that is what he offers you.

David Powlison *is the editor of the* Journal of Biblical Counseling
counseling staff at the Christian Counseling and Educational Foundation in Glenside, Pennsylvania.

RCL Ministry Booklets

Notes

Notes

COUNSELING RESOURCES

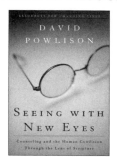

"David Powlison has profoundly impacted my ministry by teaching me the discipline of seeing life through the lens of Scripture rather than the other way around. The crumbs from Dave's table—his most casual comments— have nourished me for years. This is a feast of biblical insight."   —KEN SANDE

"Powlison urges counselors to speak directly to people rather than use abstractions. In this excellent book he takes a number of Bible passages and speaks them right into our hearts. Reading this is a rich experience for counselors and for everyone who wants to apply God's Word to his or her life."   —JOHN FRAME

COUNSELING RESOURCES

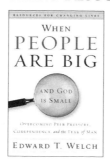

"Ed Welch is a good physician of the soul. This book is enlightening, convicting, and encouraging. I highly recommend it."

—JERRY BRIDGES

". . . refreshingly biblical. . . . brimming with helpful, readable, practical insight."

—JOHN MACARTHUR

"Readable and refreshing. . . . goes to the heart of an issue immobilizing the church. Exposes and repudiates the trivia of therapeutic theology with wisdom and compassion."

—SUSAN HUNT

COUNSELING RESOURCES

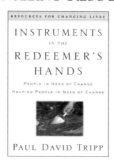

RESOURCES FOR CHANGING LIVES

INSTRUMENTS
IN THE
REDEEMER'S
HANDS

PEOPLE IN NEED OF CHANGE
HELPING PEOPLE IN NEED OF CHANGE

PAUL DAVID TRIPP

"A wonderful reminder that everyone who belongs to Jesus can help others. God gave us to each other! This is a wise and helpful book that should change your life and that of the church. Read it! You'll be glad."

—STEVE BROWN

"Tripp is a careful and skillful physician of the heart. He unites a loving heart with a mind trained to the Scriptures. This book is a great companion for pastors and counselors. It will guide anyone who wants to give real help to others, the saving help that is found in Christ's redeeming work."

—RICHARD D. PHILLIPS

COUNSELING RESOURCES

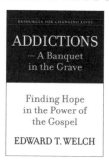

"Biblically sound, practical, filled with Christ-like compassion. . . . This much-needed book offers real hope and the promise of victory in Jesus to those struggling with addiction."

—ROBERT A. EMBERGER, Whosoever
Gospel Mission

"This is vital reading for church leaders, and for friends and family desiring to help those struggling with addictions."

—JOHN FREEMAN, HARVEST USA